I0062935

"Paul Baird has already proven to me repe̶a̶[...] are good at what they do and why some are g̶[...] one who prides yourself in being reassured that you've made the right choice, that all options have been considered, and no money has been left on the table, without any regret, then put this book on your reading list. Even after selling over $2.5 billion dollars in real estate myself, I continue to benefit from the helpful principles provided in this book. It's made a lasting impact on the way I invest and guide other people to making a confident decision."

–Zandra Ulloa,

ABR & MRP, Realtor & Founder of Team Z Realty

"I have known Paul for over ten years and worked on countless transactions with him. His sellers are always very relaxed and confident because Paul is upfront and honest about the transaction. I know that if Paul sends me a contract, he has applied the principles in this book and the property will close on time and for the agreed sales price. Paul truly wants what is best for each seller and works diligently to get the transaction to the finish line. I refer as many clients to him as I can and know that they will be in good hands. I can't recommend him enough."

–Shanae Welsh,

Escrow officer, 20 plus years experience

"Any homeowner considering a cash offer should read The Perfect Cash Offer: A Step-by-Step Guide to Selling Smart and Stress-Free for Cash. The nine principles outlined in the book are simple, straightforward, and informative."

–Brennan H. Moss,

Real Estate Attorney

"As a former IRS agent, I can appreciate the principles shared in this book. Not only are they direct and to the point, Paul does a great job of pulling back the curtains and sharing with the world that all cash buyers are not created equal. Apply these principles to any real estate transaction, and you will be better off for it."

–Benjamin Rucker,

EA, MST, Rucker Tax & Consulting LLC

"Anyone struggling with knowing how to best evaluate Cash Offers will finally have a useful resource to confidently move forward knowing they have considered all angles."

–Teryn Mozaffari,

Transaction Consultant and Certified High-Performance Coach

"The Perfect Cash Offer: A Step-by-Step Guide to Selling Smart and Stress-Free for Cash *by Paul Baird is a game-changer for anyone navigating the complex world of real estate. Paul is a seasoned real estate investor who walks you through nine crucial steps with clarity and transparency, ensuring you make informed decisions. From identifying legitimate cash buyers to minimizing contingencies, Paul's insights are a beacon of guidance. If selling your home for cash is on your mind, this book is your invaluable ally for an stress-free journey."*

–Joshua Massieh,

Real Estate Broker, Lender, and Investor

"I've worked with homeowners for over 37 years and this book really explains the alternatives to sellers who didn't know they had other options when it comes to selling their home. With an emphasis on time and money, this book takes the "scary" out of the decision-making process and gives home sellers a checklist of what to look for and what questions to ask!"

–Carolyn Church,

Escrow Officer

Trusted by thousands of homeowners to sell with confidence and peace of mind.

APPROVED
★ ★ ★
1-800 BUY-HOUSES®
★ ★ ★
OFFER

THE PERFECT CASH OFFER

A STEP-BY-STEP GUIDE TO SELLING SMART AND STRESS-FREE FOR CASH

"Because not all cash offers are created equal."

The Perfect Cash Offer: A Step-by-Step Guide to Accepting the Right Cash Offer for Your Home

Copyright © 2025 Paul Baird

2nd edition

No part of this work may be reproduced or transmitted in any form or by any means, electronic or mechanical, including photocopying and recording, or by any information storage or retrieval system, except as may be expressly permitted by the 1976 Copyright Act or in writing from the publisher. Requests for permission should be directed to paulbaird@1800BuyHouses.com.

Published by 1-800BuyHouses

ISBN: 979-8-9892040-2-1 Paperback
ISBN: 979-8-9892040-3-8 Ebook

DEDICATION

To Our Dad-

The Perfect Cash Offer wouldn't exist
without you.

Long before we ever bought a house, you
showed us what it means to do business the
right way: put the customer first, follow through
on your word, and treat people with respect.
Your example-both in life and in the print
shop-taught us that real success is built on
character, consistency, and hard work.

The values you lived by every day are the
foundation of this book. The principles behind
The Perfect Cash Offer-transparency, trust, and
doing right by people-are simply your lessons
put into practice.

Thank you for being our greatest example.

With love and gratitude,

Your Sons

TABLE OF CONTENTS

1

WHY SHOULD YOU CONSIDER A CASH OFFER?

"I purchased a house with my ex in hopes of starting our future together. Things didn't go the way we expected, and I left him the house, only for him to leave it abandoned. I knew this was going to ruin my credit, as I had no way of catching up on the mortgage plus my rent somewhere else. I didn't want to be stuck with this house and felt so hopeless and desperate for an answer.

Paul laid it out straight for me. He told me what steps needed to happen and what paperwork needed to be filed. I wasn't after money, and I wasn't wanting a long, drawn-out, stressful hassle of offices telling me why I couldn't do this or that. Paul did everything in regard to paperwork; all he needed was for me to sign a few things. It was literally less than a month that I wiped my hands clean and moved on with my life."

—Vanessa P.

Chances are, if you've picked up this book, you've received a text like this:

Hello! It's Ryan from ST Homes! Is there an amount that might make you part ways with 123 Maple Street? Let me know. 'Skip' to unsubscribe...

Or maybe a voicemail message like this:

Hi. We're looking to add another property to our portfolio, and your home looks like it might be a good fit. We'd love to schedule a time to talk about your home and make you a cash offer. Does this sound like something you'd be interested in? Give a call back at...

Perhaps you've seen the collection of "We buy houses" signs that tend to collect at intersections. They offer to buy ugly houses, foreclosures, and fixer-uppers quickly for cash. Or maybe you have received a postcard in the mail offering to purchase your home for cash or heard a radio or TV advertisement offering fast cash for your home.

If you're like most of the people we work with, you are skeptical about who these people are and if they can be trusted.

It's understandable; buying and selling a home can be overwhelming. There can be a lot of skepticism specifically when it comes to working with a cash homebuyer or investor.

Buying and selling a home can be overwhelming. There can be a lot of skepticism specifically when it comes to working with a cash homebuyer or investor.

> **One thing I have noticed over the last fifteen years is a lack of transparency that can be present when working with a cash homebuyer.**

That's why I wrote this book. I am in the cash offer business—in fact, over the last fifteen years, I have personally purchased more than $250 million of real estate *directly* from homeowners. It's not bragging to say I am very good at what I do, but one thing I have noticed over the last fifteen years is a lack of transparency that can be present when working with a cash homebuyer.

As the subtitle suggests, this book is a step-by-step guide to help you decide whether a cash offer is right for you. To empower you. To help you avoid the potential pitfalls of a bad offer.

LIFE'S ROADBLOCKS

The goal of this book is to give you the tools you need to make the best decision possible for your situation. And situations vary.

In my experience of working with thousands of homeowners, I have found that homeowners who are interested in a cash offer fall into one of five or six circumstances.

If you are facing one of these challenges, a cash offer may be the best option for you.

- When you **inherit a property,** the mortgage payments, taxes, and all of the possessions of your family member become yours. Your new property may not even be in the same city where you live. Being able to sell as-is will keep the inheritance a gift and not a burden.

- Perhaps you're a **tired landlord,** ready for a break. Selling your investment property could create the retirement you planned for without the hassle of dealing with tenants and collecting rent.

- The cost of **maintaining a home** isn't cheap, and over the years the home has been **neglected and uncared for.** The home isn't suitable for sale until major renovations are done. An "as-is" sale would lift the burden of homeownership and allow you to live without being overwhelmed.

- Jobs relocate, forcing you to pack up your family. Moving is stressful enough, and doing it under a work deadline only adds pressure. **You value a stress-free solution** to selling your home **instead of the uncertainty** that comes with putting your home on the market with a real estate agent.

- Perhaps you walk into work one day only to learn the company is issuing layoffs. **Potential foreclosure and other financial hardships** may be on the horizon. A quick home sale could help you **reset financially** sooner rather than later.

- Happy marriages can disappear seemingly overnight. One day you are making plans for the future, and the next, life has turned to chaos in the wake of **divorce**. Emotionally drained, you're ready to **cash out and move on.**

Selling a home is one of the biggest financial decisions most people will ever make—especially when the pressure is on and you need to make the right decision. That's where I come in.

Selling a home is one of the biggest financial decisions most people will ever make— especially when the pressure is on and you need to make the right decision.

REAL ESTATE ROADBLOCKS

Who am I? My name is Paul Baird, one of the founders of 1-800-BUY-HOUSES®. I purchased my first property in 2009. Since then I have purchased hundreds of properties with my dad and brothers. I consider myself one of the luckiest people in the world to be able to work with my family every day.

That's why we started 1-800-BUY-HOUSES®, to become a resource for homeowners so they can make the best decision possible.

I know working with family isn't always a good idea, but we make it work. One of the reasons it works is because we have a saying in our business: "Stay in your lane." That pretty much means do your job and let other people do theirs. For me, my "lane" is to find houses to buy. That means I am the one on the front lines talking with homeowners on a daily basis. I have sat at their kitchen tables during their most vulnerable moments as we discussed the best option for selling their home. It's something I absolutely love doing—creating a win-win situation in what can be an overwhelming process.

One thing I try to do is be an *advocate* for the homeowner. I feel like it is my responsibility to look out for their best interest—regardless of financial opportunity. That's why we started 1-800-BUY-HOUSES®, to become a resource for homeowners so they can make the best decision possible.

WHO DO YOU TRUST?

In a recent settlement with the Federal Trade Commission, Opendoor, an online real estate home-buying company, paid *$62 million* in penalties for misrepresenting its services and using deceptive tactics on potential homeowners.

Whether it's a publicly traded company like Opendoor, a real estate agent, or a local investor or homebuyer, it can be difficult to know who to trust.

As someone who has seen firsthand the lack of transparency and smoke and mirrors that come with some cash offers, I have personally experienced the individual who just got out of a weekend seminar and now claims to be a "cash buyer." Or the "company" that sends thousands of text messages a day to homeowners with no intent to ever purchase your property. Or the cold calls you receive from someone in a different country asking you to sell your house. And let's not forget the postcards you receive in the mail from your "local homebuyer."

These marketing tactics can threaten the credibility of legitimate cash buyers and, more importantly, steer you away from an option that might work best for you.

While there are a handful of credible cash homebuyers across the country, the intent of many so-called "cash buyers" is never to buy your house but to simply act as a middleman or "wholesaler" between buyers and sellers. They simply collect a fee for connecting a buyer and seller. Often, the intent from the beginning is to negotiate a price that works for you, sign a contract, and then re-negotiate a lower price closer to the closing date (more on that later).

Selling your home to the wrong person or company can make an already overwhelming situation even more overwhelming.

Selling your home to the wrong person or company can make an already overwhelming situation even more overwhelming. That's why it's essential that you understand the nine basic elements of a cash sale before moving forward with any real estate offer.

You never want to look back and say, "I wish I would have known that." Fortunately, with what I'm about to share, you won't.

All real estate professionals and cash offers are not created equal. It takes a true professional to execute and close on the agreed offer price, providing the seller peace of mind and certainty.

CLEARING THE ROADBLOCKS

All real estate professionals and cash offers are not created equal. It takes a true professional to execute and close on the agreed offer price, providing the seller peace of mind and certainty.

In 2009, I was exposed to the process of buying real estate at trustee sales. These sales took place when someone didn't pay their mortgage for an extended period of time, and the lender wanted their money back. The banks sell the property on the courthouse steps to anyone willing to buy the property "as-is."

I was fascinated by this process. As long as you had the cash, you could literally purchase a property one morning and be the property's legal owner by the next morning.

The amount of risk involved with a purchase like this is extremely high, but it was how I learned to purchase real estate. Drive the property in the morning, get as much information about the house and its condition, and then bid on the property with cashier's checks in hand.

To me, this is what a cash transaction was.

For over seven years, I purchased countless properties at the courthouse steps. As fewer foreclosures became available, I shifted my focus to working with homeowners directly. This became my passion—to work directly with them to create a win-win in what can be overwhelming circumstances.

Every homeowner has a unique situation. Some are under financial or some kind of emotional stress, which can make the home-selling process even more intense. I quickly came to realize that while I wanted to purchase every home I looked at, I knew that wasn't realistic.

Sometimes a cash offer is a good fit for a homeowner, and sometimes it's not. At the end of the day, I have made it my mission to be of value to homeowners in their decision-making process, regardless of whether I purchase their home or not. I hope to provide you with that same value through the words in this book.

Sometimes a cash offer is a good fit for a homeowner, and sometimes it's not.

Selling a home isn't something people do every day. It can be overwhelming—that's why I believe homeowners need an advocate, someone who is in their corner helping them make the best decision possible for their circumstances.

That's why I started 1-800-BUY-HOUSES®. Yes, we will purchase your home. (That's a working number; call it, and you might just get me!) But, more importantly, we want you to *make the right decision* when it comes to the sale of your home. We get just as much satisfaction from helping you make the best decision for your home as we do from buying it.

That's the reason for this book, to help YOU feel confident in the process and with the end result if you choose to sell to a cash homebuyer.

Ready to dive in?

Let's start by taking a look at Julia. She and her husband were looking for a cash offer that was both fair and fast—and almost missed both.

2

THE PAIN OF A BAD DEAL

"After a very long and hard process and dealing with a lot of very aggressive investment companies, Paul Baird showed up at our door...The process was easy and incredibly fast with absolutely no stress on us."

–Amanda G.

Most homeowners are exactly that—*homeowners*, not real estate experts—and often don't recognize the pitfalls that come with a cash offer. I've witnessed time and again the frustration a homeowner can experience by accepting the wrong offer. It is important when sellers are comparing various offers that they are comparing apples to apples.

The general consensus that brings homeowners to this point is the need to sell their property quickly and without the hassle often required with a traditional real estate sale.

But to do that, you have to know what the apples look like. As we saw in the last chapter, people choose to consider a cash offer for many reasons. However, the general consensus that brings homeowners to this point is the need to sell their property *quickly* and *without the hassle* often required with a traditional real estate sale.

And all too often, that goal is blurred by dollar signs.

JULIA'S STORY

I recently had the privilege to work with a client named Julia. She and her husband, David, found themselves considering several cash offers after the death of her father-in-law. Because they were not local to where the home was located, they had to take time away from their work, family, and their own home to settle the estate.

Not only were they navigating a real estate transaction, but they were also laying to rest a loved one and sorting through a lifetime of memories associated with the home.

They felt overwhelmed with their situation, and I was one of the first to show interest in the home. I offered a fair and reasonable price for the property but was by no means the highest.

They chose to go with the highest cash offer received— about $85,000 over mine. On the surface, that made sense. However, not all cash offers are created equal.

Julia—like many homeowners in this position—quickly learned that the promise of more money can cost the homeowner much more in the long run. They were looking at an offer that would end up taking more time, adding more stress, and allowing the buyer to renegotiate up until closing.

Here's Julia's story in her own words:

Not all cash offers are created equal.

Paul was one of the first to come look at my in-laws' home of forty-plus years. Not living in the area gave us a tight timeline to get it cleaned out, sold, and funded. We reached out to several potential buyers.

We initially accepted a much higher offer, but it turned out that was an extreme overbid (intentional or otherwise) that—through contract contingencies—allowed the buyer to drop their buying price dramatically and thus back out. Within a couple of days of canceling that contract, Paul had us in escrow closing just one week later.

Contingencies—or the lack thereof—do matter. Courtesy, honesty, and fairness also matter.

Thank you Paul. You helped make a very difficult and emotional situation go smoothly.

Thank you
Julia and David O.

THE MISTAKE OF MONEY

Julia and David made what initially seemed to be the most logical choice. They took an amazing offer that was significantly higher. What they failed to realize is that money isn't the *only* major consideration when evaluating a cash offer.

While money is obviously an important factor, it's not the only thing affecting the seller's bottom line. You also have to consider what it is costing you in:

- **Time**—Does the offer fit YOUR timeframe and provide certainty to you sooner rather than later?

- **Stress**—Does the buyer make the process seamless and easy?

- **Brain power**—Is the purchase agreement easy to understand?

You should be able to relax after accepting an offer. That's difficult to do when you're worried about an offer resting on contingencies and third-party financing. Avoiding these types of obstacles is the *exact* reason homeowners consider a cash sale in the first place.

This is why it is important to understand a few basic components of a cash offer and how they will affect the final outcome. Of course, you want to make as much money as possible on the sale of your home. But, as Julia learned, ignoring a few key factors can cost the seller both financial and emotional stress.

The mission of 1-800-BUY-HOUSES® is to help homeowners successfully navigate the process of accepting the right cash offer.

LAYING THE FOUNDATION

The mission of 1-800-BUY-HOUSES® is to help homeowners successfully navigate the process of accepting the right cash offer. My goal is to provide sellers transparency and peace of mind that allows them to focus on beginning a new chapter of their lives while knowing they made the best decisions for their situation. Part of that help includes giving sellers honest answers to their questions.

So let's tackle a few big questions you may be asking right now.

I get texts and calls asking me to sell my house. Are these legit?

- **Be skeptical of cold calls and texts** from investors "in your neighborhood." Often these are "buyers" who have no real intent to purchase your property. While some may be legitimate, proceed with caution.

I'm worried about getting taken advantage of. How do I know which buyer to trust?

- **Understand that the buyer is foundational.** Once you understand the motives and intent of a potential buyer, you have the keys to unlock a successful cash offer. While some of this may feel overwhelming, that's what this book is for. We will dive into the three elements to understanding the intention of a potential buyer and empower you to make the best decision—with confidence.

I want to make as much money as I can from the sale. The highest offer wins, right?

- **There are three parts of a cash offer to consider: Buyer, Money, and Time.** Each of these three areas is critical to understand in order to accept the right cash offer. And while you do want to make as much money as possible, there are other things to consider, like the emotional cost of selling a home as well as the financial cost. Both have to work together to create your ideal situation.

So let's begin to unpack these three parts one at a time.

OVERVIEW

The Three Essential Parts of a Cash Offer

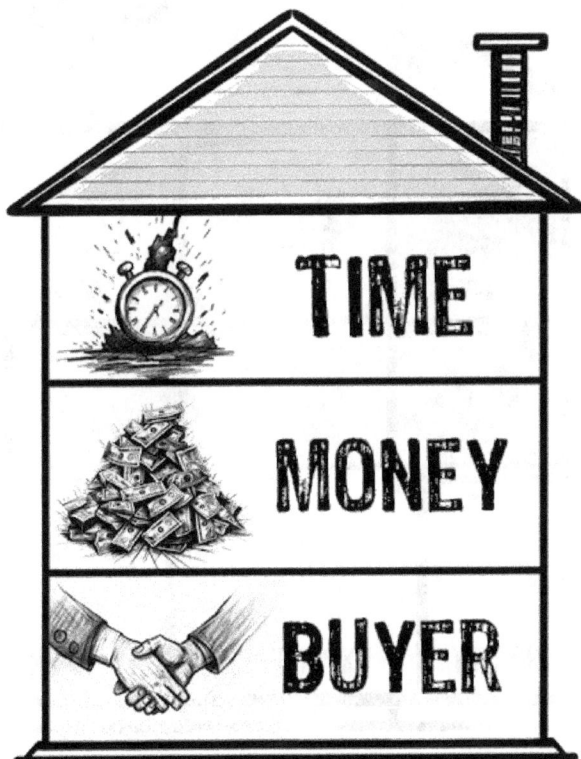

TIME

MONEY

BUYER

Taking the time to understand the potential buyer, the time it takes to close the agreement, and the money will put a seller in the best possible position to make the right decision. Each part is critical to understanding the fundamentals of a cash offer.

PART ONE

Buyer—The Offer's Foundation

Every successful cash offer must start by understanding the buyer.

Every successful cash offer must start by understanding the buyer. This forms the foundation of the sale; when you understand the buyer's intent, you will be able to better gauge the likelihood of the deal closing.

In the first part of the book, you'll learn three elements to find the right buyer:

Authority
Experience
References

An educated seller will verify the experience of the potential buyer, talk with previous clients, look at online reviews, and understand the authority and decision-making ability of the person they are working with.

PART TWO

Money: The Real Bottom Line

In the second part of the book, I'll give you three elements that will help determine the seriousness of a potential buyer and give you a clear understanding of how much money you will walk away with the day you sell the property.

Earnest Money
Net Offer
Price

The second part is understanding the specifics of both the monetary and emotional cost of selling your home.

Not understanding how these keys work together can cost you both money and emotional stress.

A wise seller needs to know how to use earnest money to *their* advantage, not the buyers', how to spot any hidden costs or fees associated with selling their home, what their real bottom line looks like, and consider both the financial cost and emotional cost of selling their home.

> **A wise seller needs to know how to use earnest money to their advantage.**

Understanding both the financial aspects and the emotional aspects of a cash offer provides sellers with the knowledge to make the best decision possible for their situation.

PART THREE

Time: Less is More

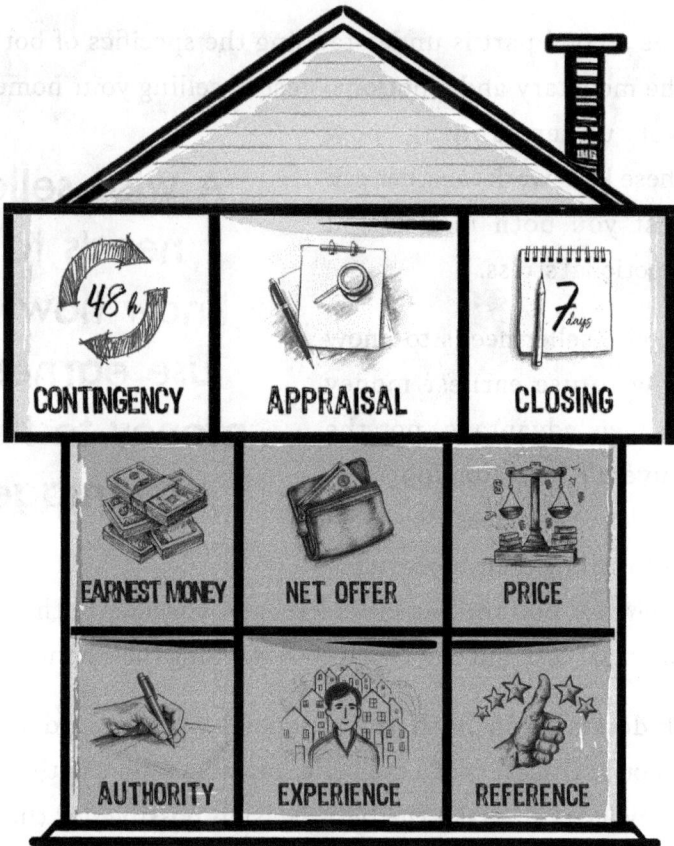

Finally, you must consider time. How much time does the buyer have to do their investigation on the property, and are they closing on *your* timeframe, not theirs? These three elements will empower you to keep the buyer accountable to your timeframe.

Contingency
Appraisal
Closing

Ben Franklin's old adage, "Time is money," has never been more true than when considering a cash offer. One of the biggest draws to selling your home to a cash buyer is the promise of a quick turnaround.

To make that happen, sellers have to avoid contingencies that slow the process and only benefit the buyer, skip time-wasters like financing conditions and appraisals, and verify the buyer can close in seven days (if needed).

Time is a valuable commodity that's difficult to put a price on. However, it can get expensive quickly if the wrong cash offer is accepted.

HERE'S HOW THE REST OF THIS BOOK IS GOING TO WORK:

To make things quick and easy for you, I've divided the information in a way that is simple to navigate. Each of the three parts and their subsequent chapters include:

- Three elements to understand the most important aspects of a cash offer

- Lists of common pitfalls and mistakes that previous sellers have made

- A checklist of action items for each key

By the time you finish, you'll be able to feel confident in your decision as you consider the best options to sell your home. My goal for you is to be empowered regardless of whether or not you accept a cash offer.

What's Next?

These elements combined will give you the understanding to *confidently* move forward with a realistic cash offer and walk away from ones that look good on paper but will likely not materialize. By the end of this book, you will be able to confidently choose the cash offer that is best for you and your particular situation.

Now, let's start with the foundation—your Buyer.

By the end of
this book, you
will be able
to confidently
choose the cash
offer that is best
for you and
your particular
situation.

PART ONE

THE BUYER

3

AUTHORITY

"Is the Buyer the True Authority Behind the Check?"

"After living there for forty-plus years, our home needed more maintenance and upgrading than we were able to undertake... 1-800-BUY-HOUSES® are investors, but by the time we were done we felt like friends."

—Marjorie M.

Everybody hates the car sales process. You work with a salesperson to pick out the car you want, then head inside to make the purchase, only to have to wait in their office while they go back and forth between you and their manager to negotiate everything from price to fees.

All this back-and-forth happens because the salesperson and the sales manager have two very different roles in the company.

The salesperson who meets you in the parking lot to show you cars is there to demonstrate the product and to convince you to buy. The manager is the one who controls the pricing and handles the business of negotiating to ensure the dealership's bottom line is met.

So, while you're sitting in the salesperson's office, he is negotiating on your behalf with the decision-maker. Do you really want the person who works for a commission in charge of making sure you get the best deal?

I would much rather talk to the person making the decision myself. Most people would.

Selling a home is no different. This is why working *directly* with the decision maker and understanding their intent is crucial to a successful cash offer.

Start by finding out exactly who is doing the walk-through of your property.

Are they an acquisitions manager? Are they a salesman or middleman who has to go back to talk to the person in charge?

Or are they the one writing the check? Do they have the authority to make the final call on purchase price and timelines?

KNOWING THE PLAYERS

There are three main players when selling your home: cash buyers, real estate agents, and wholesalers. Let's unpack real estate agents and wholesalers one by one.

CASH BUYERS

Cash Buyer

Seller ——→ Cash Buyer

The cash buyer is who you want to work with if you are reading this book. They have the authority and the ability to make a decision and purchase your home. There is no intermediary. There are no extra steps. It's the shortest path to done.

REAL ESTATE AGENTS

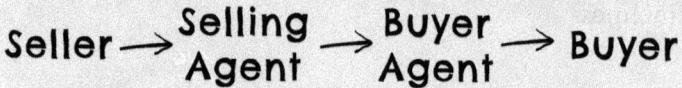

Real Estate Agent

———————————

Seller $\rightarrow$ Selling Agent $\rightarrow$ Buyer Agent $\rightarrow$ Buyer

In their simplest role, real estate agents act on behalf of sellers. They go back and forth between the buyer and seller to broker the purchase and sale of real estate.

And so, in a normal real estate transaction, there will be:

- The homeowner, who is selling
- The selling agent, who works on the seller's behalf with the buyer's agent
- The buyer, who wants to purchase the property
- The buyer's agent, who is the go-between for the buyer to the seller's agent

This can quickly turn into something like the Telephone Game if there is any breakdown in communication. Remember the old children's game where you whisper into the ear of the kid next to you? Then they repeat what you said by whispering into the ear of the person next to them, and it continues around the circle until it gets back to the person that started it.

By the time it gets to the person at the end, it's not even close to the original statement. And so, this is one of the biggest benefits of working with a cash buyer who intends to purchase your home. Why? Because you get to communicate *directly* with the one who has the ability to purchase your home.

If a real estate agent is involved with a cash offer, there are most likely commissions and other fees involved. That being said, real estate agents can be incredibly valuable in more complicated situations or where a homeowner feels comfortable. Regardless, it's important to understand what the real estate agent's role in the transaction is going to be.

Real estate agents can be incredibly valuable in more complicated situations or where a homeowner feels comfortable. Regardless, it's important to understand what the real estate agent's role in the transaction is going to be.

REAL ESTATE WHOLESALERS

Wholesaler

Seller —→ Wholesaler—→ Buyer

If you are getting text messages or phone calls from people soliciting to buy your house, or maybe you have seen an online ad that says "We buy houses," there's a really good chance that these people aren't really cash buyers. They are **wholesalers** who often market themselves as cash buyers.

A wholesaler's goal is to enter into a purchase agreement with a homeowner with the intent to sell their interest to someone else for a fee. Within that agreement, they have the right to "assign" the contract to another buyer. Essentially, they become a middleman who then sells your home to someone who actually has the cash to purchase the property.

Go online and search "sell my house for cash," "we buy houses," or anything else related to buying homes for cash. Say ten companies pop up. A majority of these companies will advertise "We buy houses for cash." However, out of those ten, maybe two or three will be *legitimate* cash buyers who have the intent and/or the ability to purchase your home.

The scary side of real estate wholesaling is that anyone can legally do it. You don't have to be a real estate agent, get a certification, or take classes.

Wholesalers can operate in most places without any specialized knowledge of the real estate market. Some of them don't know much about real estate but are very good at marketing and sales.

Wholesalers don't buy real estate yet call themselves "cash buyers" or "investors."

Over the last several years wholesaling has become an entire business model for lots of so-called "real estate investors." The interesting thing is that wholesalers don't buy real estate yet call themselves "cash buyers" or "investors." Each state regulates "wholesaling" differently. Some states are much stricter about it than others, but regardless, there is no education or experience required.

It's not uncommon for homeowners who are considering a cash offer to talk with someone who appears to know a lot about real estate, but in reality, they are just a good salesperson. That could set you up for disaster.

Let me be clear, not all wholesalers are bad; there are countless companies and individuals that run a very successful and ethical business. That being said, knowing who you are dealing with as a seller is really important to making sure you have a solid cash offer.

Take the example of a reputable company in Salt Lake City—let's call them ABC Homebuyer. They have helped facilitate thousands of people selling their houses, but they have acted as a wholesaler more than an actual cash buyer. There are thousands of wholesale companies across the country that do this, and it's completely legal.

When a seller visits a wholesaler website, they will see advertisements like, "Sell your home as-is," "We pay cash," "We buy houses fast," or "We buy houses." There will be promises of getting an as-is cash offer directly from ABC Homebuyer to close in as little as seven days.

That would be very similar to what our 1800BUYHOUSES.com website says—"Sell your house fast." We pay cash, too. So from a seller's perspective, whether it's 1800BUYHOUSES.com or ABC Homebuyer, sellers see the companies as doing the exact same thing.

While it looks the same on the surface, that is actually not the case. What ABC Homebuyer is doing isn't buying your house at all, they are actually looking to sell the property to someone else; it's called assigning the contract.

So, ABC Homebuyer goes to a seller and offers to buy their house for cash. The seller accepts the offer and they sign an agreement for ABC Homebuyer to buy the property.

However, in this contract, the seller gives ABC Homebuyer the right to *assign* the contract. You will typically find this in one of the following places in the purchase agreement.

After the buyer's name, it will read "and/or assignees."

Or there will be a section of the purchase agreement called "Assignments," and it will read something like this:

> *Purchaser shall have the right to assign this Agreement or any of Purchaser's rights hereunder. In the event of an assignment of this Agreement, Purchaser reserves the right to receive value for said assignment, which may be greater than the purchase price.*

Since most sellers are just reading the highlights, they don't realize this gives ABC Homebuyer the right to *assign* this contract to someone else.

Oftentimes, there is no intent for ABC Homebuyer to actually purchase the home.

ASSIGNING THE CONTRACT

After the contract is signed, the ABC Homebuyer representative goes back to his office, where he has an email list of potential buyers. He sends an email saying he has an **assignable contract** to purchase a property, which he will sell for X amount of dollars.

So, ABC Homebuyer is trying to sell the property he has agreed to purchase to another buyer *who actually has the money*. Keep in mind ABC Homebuyer has not yet actually purchased the property from the seller, he's just signed an agreement that he *intends* to do so.

ABC Homebuyer contract with homeowner	Assignment fee	Cash buyer purchase price
$525,000	$25,000	$550,000

As you can see, ABC Homebuyer doesn't have much intent to purchase the property; they are looking to make an **assignment fee**. These fees can range from as little as $2,500 to as high as $100,000. Here is an example of what that looks like.

ABC Homebuyer agrees to purchase your home for $525,000. Back at the office, ABC Homebuyer contacts their list of buyers and markets the property for $550,000. ABC Homebuyer hopes to make the difference between the purchase agreement price with the seller and what they market the property for, in this case, $25,000.

If someone on ABC Homebuyer's list is interested in the property, then that person will be the one who actually purchases the property from the seller on the day the property closes. As you can see, ABC Homebuyer never purchased the property but simply sold their interest in the deal for a fee.

This can cause problems for the seller because they are not actually working with the person who is going to buy the property.

As someone who has seen this scenario thousands of times, there are two problems:

Number One: A Renegotiated Price.

If another buyer doesn't want to pay $550,000 for the property, what is the wholesaler going to do? They're either going to reduce their fee or they're going to renegotiate the purchase price with the seller.

To protect their own bottom line, the wholesaler usually renegotiates the purchase price with the seller.

To protect their own bottom line, the wholesaler usually renegotiates the purchase price with the seller. Instead of the seller getting $525,000 for the property the new purchase price could be 500,000, reducing the amount of money the seller gets by $25,000.

This is why wholesalers want extra time built into their contracts through contingencies. We'll talk more about these in Part Three. For now, just know these are clauses written into the contract giving the buyer a way out of the agreement. These contingencies give the wholesalers time to sell the property to someone else.

This is the reason 1-800-BUY-HOUSES® believes in a 48-hour contingency (more on that later).

Number Two: A Lack of Transparency.

The seller has no idea what is happening behind the scenes. Many wholesalers include an inspection period in the contract. They'll say, "I need some contractors to come by and look at the property during this inspection period." This is a red flag.

If their "business partners" come by, that's another red flag. After the purchase agreement is signed, the wholesaler will ask the buyer if he can take some videos and pictures of the property for his "partners" and "contractors." These videos and pictures will be the ones he uses in the email when he markets the property for $549,000.

Along with taking videos and pictures, the wholesaler will ask the buyer if there is a day he could have his "partners" or "contractors" do an inspection of the property. It seems like a reasonable request, but it's all smoke and mirrors. What is actually happening is the wholesaler is setting up a time for potential buyers to walk through the property.

Meanwhile, the seller doesn't know any better and lets the process play out.

I have seen twenty to thirty potential buyers walk through a property that a wholesaler is trying to sell. It's unethical and disingenuous to the seller. In many cases, the seller contacted a cash buyer to avoid the exact situation the wholesaler has put them in, home walkthroughs and inspections, but by this time it's too late to do anything because they have already signed a contract.

Homeowners call cash buyers to avoid situations like this. They don't want to deal with the traditional process. They aren't interested in the time, work, and effort real estate agents require in the traditional process of selling a property.

RED FLAGS

- Accepting a legitimate cash offer from a buyer with authority doesn't have to be painful. But to be sure you are making a wise decision, pay attention to these red flags.

- The more directly you can work with the actual buyer the better off you will be as the seller. Be hesitant to work directly with anyone but the final decision maker.

- Avoid contracts that are "assignable" to another person, entity or company.

- Anytime a potential buyer in the cash-offer world says, "my business partners" "my associates," "my contractor" it could denote working with a wholesaler.

- Be cautious of allowing anyone to take photos and videos of your home.

THE BIG IDEA UNLOCKED

- As a seller, it's important to recognize what an authentic cash buyer looks like. Be cautious of talking to wholesalers or anyone else whose intention with the property is questionable. You want to talk with someone who has the authority and ability to purchase your property.

4

EXPERIENCE

"Has the Buyer Been There Before?"

"Paul came out the next day and got me an offer the same night. I had several others come by...only to not send me an offer as requested, low-ball the offer, or make promises through a contract that wouldn't hold any guarantees."

—Damian

C an you imagine asking your neighbor, whose favorite channel is the Food Network, to bake you a wedding cake for your big day? Or asking your buddy, who fixed a flat tire, to replace your transmission? Or a doctor fresh out of med school to take a look at your heart?

These examples may seem extreme, but that's exactly what happens if you don't work with an experienced cash homebuyer. The purchase or sale of real estate is one of the biggest financial decisions you will ever make.

Why would you not ask how experienced a potential **cash buyer** is? An inexperienced cash buyer can cost you time, money, and more stress in what's meant to be a quick, stress-free process.

Working with a cash buyer should be simple, and with an experienced buyer, it will be. Sadly, I've known many sellers who think the property is going to close in a few days until the buyer either renegotiates the purchase price or walks away from the purchase of the home altogether.

It is not uncommon for sellers to have the sale of a home fall apart days before the expected closing date due to the buyer.

Legitimate cash buyers are able to move quickly. They can easily assess the market, estimate any potential repair costs, and determine whether or not you might be a good fit for a cash offer.

An
inexperienced
cash buyer
can cost you
time, money,
and more
stress in what's
meant to be a
quick, stress-
free process.

Working with an experienced cash buyer who you can trust will prove to be a priceless resource.

Inexperienced buyers often put themselves at an advantage by giving themselves the right to walk away from the purchase agreement at any time, without consequence, leaving the seller in a position to start the entire process over again.

Albert Einstein said, "If you can't explain it simply, you don't understand it well enough." An experienced cash buyer will be able to walk you through the process of selling your home step-by-step, making something that can often be complicated easy and straightforward.

Selling a home isn't something people do every day. Working with an experienced cash buyer who you can trust will prove to be a priceless resource.

You may be asking, *How am I supposed to know an experienced cash homebuyer when I see one?* This first part is designed to help you look past the slick-talking salesman and help you identify who actually has the intent to purchase your home versus someone who may intend to wholesale your home.

The more houses someone has previously purchased, the more credibility they have as a buyer.

To avoid getting handcuffed by a purchase agreement that significantly favors the buyer, carefully prequalify two or three potential buyers by asking them some very direct questions:

- How long have you been buying real estate?
- Tell me about the last two houses you purchased.
- What do you do with the properties you purchase?
- What is your title/position with the company?
- Do you intend to wholesale my property?

Selling your home is a legal transaction. Even if you meet with your friend's favorite nephew—who they assure you is a qualified professional—*do your homework*. You won't insult a true professional by asking questions and doing research.

The more houses someone has previously purchased, the more credibility they have as a buyer. They know what to look out for, how to prevent delays, and have the experience necessary to navigate any potential roadblocks.

An experienced cash homebuyer has the skill set to walk through your property one time, evaluate the layout and condition, and give you an offer within twenty-four hours. They will already have a title and escrow company or real estate attorney (depending on the state) they have worked with in the past that will help both the buyer and seller through the entire transaction.

A less experienced buyer or someone who is an acquisitions specialist for a bigger company may tell you what you want to hear about the price, but in the end, it costs you more time and money than necessary. They tend to be better salesmen than they are real estate investors.

You may also want to think twice about working with someone buying real estate as a side gig. Chances are they have a full-time job and other obligations. This could potentially slow down the sales process.

Just as if you were going into surgery you would choose the doctor who has done a lot of surgeries versus the surgeon just out of medical school, you want an experienced cash buyer you can trust and depend on.

The more experienced the buyer, the more likely you are to receive a rock-solid offer.

RECOGNIZE EXPERIENCE

Start by asking how many cash transactions they have made in the last year, and ask for the addresses of a few of those properties. Search those properties online and see if they have been recently purchased or sold. Sites like Zillow and Redfin can be a good resource.

Your goal is to work with someone who not only understands real estate but has experience purchasing homes for cash.

Your goal is to work with someone who not only understands real estate but has experience purchasing homes for cash. The process is much faster when you aren't working with many of the traditional aspects of selling a home. Make sure the buyer can do what he or she says they can do.

Asking questions and getting to know your potential buyer will prove to be essential in making the right decision. It can ease any doubts and help build trust through the process.

The more experienced the buyer, the more likely you are to receive a rock-solid offer.

RED FLAGS

Remember Einstein's advice. You're looking for a buyer who has experience and can not only explain the process in a simple manner but can execute. You may want to consider moving on to the next buyer if your buyer:

- Has never purchased a property before.

- Lacks confidence and seems unsure of the process.

- Is pushy, making you feel like you are being sold something and pressured.

THE BIG IDEA UNLOCKED

- Always follow up! Verify that what they are telling you is true. Remember, your goal is to walk away with peace of mind that you got a fair offer.

- Make sure your prospective buyer has the skill set to do what they say they are going to do; this comes through experience. This will ensure the process runs smoothly and according to the timeframe you set forth in the purchase agreement.

- An experienced cash homebuyer has the skill set to walk through your property one time, evaluate the layout and condition, and give you an offer within twenty-four hours.

5

REFERENCE

"Does the Buyer Have High Character and Good References?"

"*I found Paul through a Google search. I read all the reviews and decided I would contact them. I'm so grateful I did. All the positive reviews are accurate, and I would definitely recommend them.*"

—Debbie S.

Are you the type of person who likes to ask for a recommendation for a restaurant? Or a reference for a mechanic? Even buying something on Amazon—you scroll down and look at ratings and reviews.

There are entire websites devoted to giving recommendations for everything from contractors to dentists to pizza parlors. You see on social media all the time someone asking their friends to recommend a handyman, landscaper, caterer, or babysitter.

Good decision-making is based on information and experience.

The more important—or more expensive—the task, the more hesitant people are to trust it to a stranger.

So, why wouldn't you do your due diligence on contacting someone who is an expert in handling one of the largest financial transactions you'll face? Good decision-making is based on information and experience. Since most sellers are not experts, they need to rely on cash homebuyers who are.

But how do you narrow the field down to a qualified homebuyer when everyone seems to be saying the same thing?

Let's face it—some people talk a good game with very few results. Don't get stuck working with a homebuyer who hasn't been around enough to have made the contacts, learned the ropes, or established a name for themselves in the field.

Don't get stuck
working with
a homebuyer
who hasn't been
around enough
to have made
the contacts,
learned the ropes,
or established
a name for
themselves in
the field.

This element is short and sweet: trust, but verify.

Start with a Google search to see what kind of reviews are out there about different cash homebuyers and their businesses. Do they have an online presence? Do they have any reviews? Are they positive? If there are negatives, what are they? How many reviews are there? A few negative reviews out of hundreds doesn't necessarily mean anything bad. But, three out of ten reviews is a different story altogether.

Next, check the references of your prospective buyer. Ask for names of past clients, then ask to talk to them. Find out what the client's experience was like and if the buyer did what they said they were going to do.

It is also important to make sure the buyer is compatible with your needs as a seller. Checking references can help you understand:

- The buyer's qualifications
- Their special areas of expertise
- Whether or not they were truthful in the information they provided you
- How well they work under time constraints
- Their personality and work style

I have offered to let sellers speak to former clients like Julia from Chapter Two. I explain to them that Julia's been through this process and she could probably provide some pretty good information about what the process was like vetting and talking to different cash buyers.

It's not offensive to ask to check references, and professionals are always happy to provide them.

If you have concerns, I would recommend you call the escrow and title company. They are a third-party company that's going to help handle the transactions. They are the ones who will do the title search on the property and handle the money. They're going to make sure both the buyer and the seller do what they're supposed to do.

> **It's not offensive to ask to check references, and professionals are always happy to provide them.**

When you call the title company, say something along the lines of, "I'm working with XYZ buyers. What's your experience with this individual or company? Do they close a lot of properties with you?"

The escrow and title company should be more than happy to share their experience with that particular buyer.

These are a few specific things a seller can do to verify the legitimacy of a buyer. Take a magnifying glass to these things:

- **Past clients**—You want first-hand experience from real clients. Who have the buyers worked with before, and what impression did they leave?

- **Google reviews**—These are a little less trustworthy, but still a great way to learn more about prospective buyers. Are the positive/ negative reviews proportionate to the number of reviewers?

- **Title and escrow company**—An experienced buyer will have a good working relationship with other businesses in the industry. Learn more about their relationships with the people they work with the most. Are they able to confirm they have worked with the buyer previously? Was it a positive experience?

- **Online presence**—Do they have a website and seem credible? Are they on social media and seem to have helped other people in a similar situation as yours?

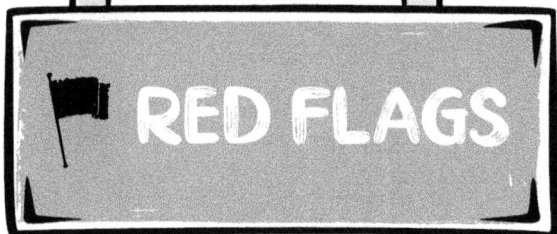

RED FLAGS

- No online reviews or presence.

- Title and escrow company not willing to share basic information.

- Not willing to let you talk to previous clients.

A legitimate company doesn't just look legitimate—they can back it up. Make sure they don't just talk a good game; they should actually demonstrate success by pointing you to others who will vouch for them.

- It's okay to trust people but still verify what they're saying is true. Selling a home deals with tens of thousands of dollars and shouldn't be treated lightly. Check the prospective buyer's references. Talk to the title company they work with. Read through their online reviews and evaluate their overall online presence and social media. Take the time to check that they are who they claim to be and can be trusted based on their past experience.

A legitimate
company doesn't just
look legitimate–they
can back it up.

PART ONE PUNCH LIST

Key Takeaways

- The more experienced the buyer, the more likely you are to receive a legitimate offer.

- Trust, but verify. Use buyer references from past clients, Google reviews, and talk to the title and escrow company.

- Understand who you are working with: a wholesaler, real estate agent, or cash buyer.

PART ONE RED FLAGS

- When a seller asks the buyer how long they have been in business, and the buyer's answer includes other people, it is a complete Red Flag.

- Anytime a potential buyer in the cash-offer world says, "my business partners" or "my associates," it could denote they are not the true cash buyer, but a third party. It could also hint toward the fact that they personally do not have much experience and do not have much knowledge about the cash-buying process.

- Look out for language that hints at a lack of experience or reliance on other people to do the job.

- Watch out for buyers who can't explain the cash-buying process in simplified terms.

- Beware of buyers who bring in business partners, inspectors, or contractors. Both are common ways wholesalers allow other cash buyers to see the property.

- Be cautious of signing a purchase agreement that allows the buyer to assign the contract.

Want to learn more about the Buyer's role in a cash offer?

Scan the QR code to watch Paul's video.

SCAN ME

PART TWO

THE MONEY

MONEY

6

EARNEST MONEY

"Is the Buyer Willing to Put a Little Skin in the Game?"

"Once we agreed on a price, and signed the title, money was in our account within twenty-four hours."

—Jutta K.

What would a store manager say if you gathered their best-selling items and left them with the cashier with a promise you'll come back to buy them? They probably wouldn't let that happen.

They don't know you, have no guarantee you'll come back, and have other customers willing to make the purchase at that moment. There's a reason retailers don't operate this way. They'd quickly go out of business if paying customers couldn't get what they wanted because prospective buyers were tying up the products.

As a homeowner, why would you operate this way?

Signing a purchase agreement with very little or no **earnest money** offers you no guarantees or reassurances. In fact, it could cause you to lose time with more risk of the purchase not going through.

Buyers can effectively take your property off the market as they are still deciding if they want to purchase it or not—at no risk to them. It's not fair to the sellers or other buyers.

Let's look at it this way:

XYZ Cash Buyer makes you an offer for your home and you accept. The two of you sign an agreement, but there is no earnest money. AAA Homebuyer contacts you about your property, but you explain you've already signed an agreement with XYZ Cash Buyer.

Earnest money can be a game-changer for sellers.

XYZ Cash Buyer then decides he's changed his mind about the purchase—perhaps he is trying to wholesale the property to another buyer and can't pay what he originally offered, so he wants to renegotiate the purchase price. This is obviously frustrating for you, and when the offer falls through, you feel like you have been taken advantage of.

Meanwhile, AAA Homebuyer, who offered non-refundable earnest money at the time of acceptance could have saved you the frustration and time of working with someone with very little commitment to purchase the property. You've wasted time and money on XYZ. Meanwhile, XYZ Cash Buyer hasn't lost anything and is free to walk away with no consequences.

Earnest money can be a game-changer for sellers. But for it to work, the seller needs to know three things about earnest money when it comes to real estate:

1. What it is and when it comes into play
2. Why it's important
3. How much should be required

EARNEST MONEY: THE WHAT AND WHEN

Earnest Money Deposit, or EMD, is a good-faith deposit given by the buyer to the seller. It's an amount of money that tells the seller a buyer is serious about purchasing the home. Other terms you may see are good-faith deposit and escrow deposit.

Once a purchase agreement is signed, the buyer typically has three to five days to take the earnest money deposit to the title company or a real estate attorney to be held in escrow. If the buyer backs out of the agreement for reasons other than what's listed in the contract, the seller is entitled to the earnest money.

These funds encourage buyers to follow through on the purchase agreement.

The earnest money will be held in escrow until the closing date. If the transaction goes as agreed upon, the earnest money will go towards the purchase price of the property.

Earnest money typically comes into play when there are contingencies or clauses written into the contract. We will get more into contingencies in Part Three. For now, it's important to know that earnest money is a major indicator of how serious a buyer is to purchase the property.

THE IMPORTANCE OF GOOD FAITH

The purpose of earnest money when considering any offer on real estate is to gauge how serious the potential buyer is; this becomes even more important when considering a cash offer. It gives the seller confidence in the buyer's commitment to doing business, especially if they are willing to put non-refundable earnest money in the purchase agreement.

The purpose of earnest money when considering any offer on real estate is to gauge how serious the potential buyer is.

The more earnest money a potential buyer puts down strengthens the offer and ultimately builds trust between the buyer and seller.

- It shows how serious the buyer is.
- It protects the seller from the buyer backing out of the purchase.
- It protects the interest of both parties because it shows the willingness of the seller to sell and the seriousness of the buyer to buy.

As you can see, both parties benefit from an earnest money deposit.

The higher
the non-
refundable
earnest
money,
the more
serious
the buyer.

SO HOW MUCH SHOULD IT BE?

While there is no set formula for how much earnest money should be given, it's not just some arbitrary number. Take time to consider a few important points about the amount:

- Earnest Money can range from 1-5% of the purchase price, which will eventually be used toward the purchase price of the home.

- As the seller, you want the earnest money amount to be high enough that the buyer has skin in the game. The goal is to keep the buyer from canceling the purchase agreement for no legitimate reason.

Understanding the purpose of Earnest Money up front gives the seller a greater sense of comfort that they are working with a serious buyer. **The higher the non-refundable earnest money, the more serious the buyer.**

For example, if XYZ Cash Buyer is purchasing a property for $850,000, and puts down 5%, that's $42,500. That's a significant amount that XYZ Cash Buyer is less likely to walk away from.

On the other hand, if XYZ Cash Buyer only puts down $2,550, that is significantly less. That's only .3% of the purchase price and a lot easier to swallow if he walks away.

That said, as long as the amount is enough that it makes the buyer second guess walking away from the purchase agreement for no legitimate reason, the amount is sufficient.

Here's how you know that you're working with a serious cash buyer: ask them for non-refundable earnest money at the time the offer is accepted.

NO REFUNDS

Here's how you know that you're working with a serious cash buyer: ask them for non-refundable earnest money at the time the offer is accepted. At the very least, earnest money should be non-refundable after all contingencies are removed—ideally within forty-eight hours of purchase.

Why? Because that requires them to put some skin in the game.

When a consumer buys a product or service from a store with a No Return/No Refund policy, they tend to be more certain about the purchase.

No matter how much buyer's remorse they have, they can't take the product back. The same policy applies here. Make sure the buyer understands that you are only interested in working with cash buyers who are willing to put their money where their mouth is.

As a cash homebuyer, I typically put $10,000-$20,000 non-refundable earnest money forward at the time my offer is accepted. That means from the moment the seller and I sign that agreement, they would be entitled to the $10,000 earnest money if I don't follow through.

Require non-refundable earnest money when considering a cash offer, regardless of the amount. It will provide peace of mind knowing the buyer is serious and plans to follow through with their end of the agreement.

RED FLAGS

- Any sales agreement where $0 earnest money is put down is a serious red flag that someone is not an experienced buyer.

- Another red flag comes when the buyer can't or won't show Proof of Funds.

- No earnest money means a buyer can walk away from their cash offer at any time without consequence right up until the day the property is scheduled to close. The buyer risks nothing on this offer; the seller risks everything.

- If a buyer only puts down a small percentage of the purchase, it presents a higher risk to the seller.

- If you are working with somebody who seems like a promising buyer, but they don't want the earnest money to be nonrefundable, walk away.

THE BIG IDEA UNLOCKED

- Knowing that the higher the earnest money, the more serious the buyer empowers the seller to make educated decisions when accepting an offer. A seller receiving multiple cash offers will be able to weed through and know who the legitimate buyers are rather quickly.

- This whole key is about the buyer putting their money where their mouth is. When it comes to earnest money, the buyer's goal should be to always create more certainty for the seller.

7

NET

"Do You Have All the Information to Make an Informed Decision?"

"We received a legitimate cash offer in one day, with no contingencies, near the net sales price we would have received had we tried to sell with a traditional real estate agent. We avoided a lot of the waiting and hassle associated with showings. This worked out great for our situation of needing to sell quickly."

—Matthew N.

There is just something about putting on a coat or pair of pants and finding forgotten cash in your pocket. For some reason, it's exhilarating, even when it's only a dollar or two. Suddenly the day is brighter, and we can treat ourselves to some small pleasure.

Contrast that with the sting that comes from realizing you've lost money. Perhaps you misplaced the cash to pay back a friend for lunch, didn't collect your change from the cashier, or can't find the $20 that was on the table.

When you don't keep up with your cash, you don't tend to have it for long.

In my experience working with sellers, they just want to know how much money they're going to walk away with.

Most people are all about the top dollar and bottom line. The truth is, though, most don't take the time to understand the details of the costs versus benefits when considering a cash offer.

Your property is one of your biggest assets. You have to treat it as such, especially when considering selling your home.

In my experience working with sellers, they just want to know how much money they're going to walk away with.

Before you can make an accurate calculation, you have to know your total debt. These debts may include mortgages, liens, taxes, or judgments that would need to be paid from the proceeds of the sale.

Selling a home isn't something people do every day, so understanding some of the details of how the sales process works when it comes to money is important.

This chapter exists to explain to sellers how to determine the **net proceeds** from the sale of their home. Many think they walk away pocketing the sales price. But the reality can be much different.

For example, you may sell your home for $100,000 on the market through a real estate agent, but that does not mean you walked away with $100,000 in your pocket.

Let's walk through the two scenarios: a traditional sale and a cash sale.

Before you can make an accurate calculation, you have to know your total debt. These debts may include mortgages, liens, taxes, or judgments that would need to be paid from the proceeds of the sale.

Once you know these numbers, you can compare a traditional sale to a cash offer.

TRADITIONAL SALE

The first scenario to consider is selling a property on the market with a real estate agent. These are the kinds of home sales you might see on Zillow, Redfin, or the local **MLS (Multi-Listing Service)**. In almost all of these sales, there is a cost associated with selling the property. According to

Zillow, one of real estate's most trusted resources, the cost of selling a home can range from 6-10%.

THE AVERAGE COST OF SELLING A HOME

- **Agent Fees** 5-6%

  Title Insurance ...... 0.05-1% Purchase Price

  Escrow Fees .... 1-2% of Purchase Price

  Transfer Tax .... Varies by State

  Attorney Fees .... Varies by State

  Prorated Property Taxes .... Prorated Up to Close

  HOA Fees .... Prorated Up to Close

If you sell your home for $100,000, plan to subtract around 10%.

That percentage includes the 5-6% commission for the seller's and buyer's agents. There are also closing costs associated with the title, settlement, and taxes. Keep in mind these numbers do not include any costs related to preparing the home for listing, repairs, seller concessions, or moving.

You can see there may be several different costs associated with selling a property on the market that all add up. A seller who sells for $100,000 will see their net proceeds around $93,000 (at best) *before* paying any outstanding debts (i.e. mortgage, back taxes, etc.)

The seller who accepts a legitimate cash offer shouldn't have to pay real estate commissions and/or any costs associated with selling the property.

CASH SALE

Now let's consider the second scenario from a cash buyer. The typical cash buyer advertises that the seller will not be responsible for any fees or commissions associated with the sale of the property. So if that's the case, if a cash buyer offers $93,000 using the same example above, those two offers are the same, meaning the seller's net will be the same.

The seller who accepts a legitimate cash offer shouldn't have to pay real estate commissions and/or any costs associated with selling the property.

As a seller, it's important to understand the costs associated with the sale of the property so that you know what your net will be.

OpenDoor, a full service real estate iBuyer, was fined by the FTC because they *misrepresented* how much closing costs would be for the seller, giving sellers *a false estimate* of how much money they would actually walk away with.

Whether OpenDoor misled customers or not, I don't know. What I do know is that if sellers better understood this process, fewer people would have been taken advantage of.

IMPORTANT NUMBERS TO KNOW

You don't have to know exact amounts, but before entertaining a cash offer, it's good to understand some ballpark figures of what to expect. To determine a good estimate of how much money you will get from the sale of your house, you will need to know:

- What fees will be coming out of your proceeds at closing?

- What costs (if any) are you expected to cover?

- How much is owed on your home's mortgage, property taxes, judgments, etc.?

Knowing these numbers can help you figure out your net proceeds. The equation is straightforward for a traditional sale; however, remember the chart above and how much comes out before you reach your net.

Traditional Sale Vs. Cash Sale

OFFER PRICE

- Closing Costs (1-2%)
- Commissions (5-6%)
- Debt (mortgage, liens, judgments)

= Net

OFFER PRICE

- Debt (mortgage, liens, judgments)

= Net

This will give you a pretty good idea of how much you can expect to make from the sale. Never accept an offer without knowing these basic numbers.

Never accept an offer without knowing these basic numbers.

RED FLAGS

- The finances of real estate can be intimidating, so don't hesitate to ask questions.

- Ask what fees you will be paying, then follow up by getting an explanation for charges you're not sure about.

- Look out for anything a buyer says is "just a normal cost of selling" or "typical fees" without any real breakdown of what they mean.

- Double-check the numbers the buyer is giving you. Be cautious of individuals or companies who can't give you an estimate of your net proceeds based on the offer amount.

THE BIG IDEA UNLOCKED

- Selling for cash means no realtor commissions, fees, closing costs, inspections, appraisals, extended timeframe, or showings. There shouldn't be any extras coming off your offer. Here's an easy way to remember what your NET stands for: No Extra Things.

- A buyer's offer price is what the seller will walk away with minus any debt. That total is what you should expect to walk away with the day the property closes.

- When you know your net, you ensure you can make an educated decision about which offer to accept and eliminate any surprises at closing.

When you know
your net, you
ensure you
can make an
educated decision
about which
offer to accept
and eliminate
any surprises
at closing.

8

PRICE

"Have You Considered the Emotional Cost of the Sale?"

"Paul offered us above what our 'bottom line' was... We didn't have the headache of listing, inspection, or any of the other typical selling hassles. We just signed and received payment."

—Wendy N.

The emotional price is very real and should be considered when determining the seller's bottom line.

Nobody wants to overpay for a purchase. Everyone expects to pay a fair price and be treated with respect.

Today's consumers have a world of information at their fingertips. It's all online. Comparing offers and finding deals has never been easier. Bargain-hunting shoppers have been known to go to great lengths to get their purchase at just the right price.

We've seen the lines and throngs of people shopping on Black Friday. More than a few people make the news each year for carrying their hunt for savings a little too far.

PRICE

For better or for worse, this dynamic carries over into real estate. While the buyer and seller both want to create a win-win situation, it can be a little tricky to determine exactly what *fair* is.

Buyers often think in terms of dollars and cents—their bottom line. Sellers, on the other hand, are typically looking at two factors: the amount of money they are going to walk away with (*their* bottom line) and the *emotional* cost of selling the property, both of which equal the price of selling a home.

Whether sellers are driven by emotional attachment, the stress of moving, or any of life's roadblocks listed in Chapter One, the **emotional price** is very real and should be considered when determining the seller's bottom line. For the seller, it's about finding a balance between the emotional cost and the financial cost.

So, when it comes to setting a price for a successful sale, what's a seller to do?

The financial part of the balance is easy to figure out because it is simply the price someone is willing to pay.

Remember your net offer equation:

Offer Price – Debt = Net

This is one side of the balance. The other side of the balance is a bit more complicated.

TWO PRICES, ONE HOUSE

You don't sell a home for cash in an effort to get top dollar. Selling a home for cash means it's priced fairly, but also takes into consideration other roadblocks that are driving the sale of your home.

> You don't sell a home for cash in an effort to get top dollar.

The other side of the balance is the **Emotional Price or Cost.** Most people choose to work with a cash buyer over a traditional sale because there are emotional factors at play. It's not uncommon for homeowners to trade money for convenience.

Let's consider the situation of a seller I recently spoke with who lives in Florida and is helping her elderly mother sell her house in Salt Lake City. The mother wants to move to Florida to be near her daughter.

However, before that can happen, they need to sell Mom's house in Utah over 2,000 miles away. Mom has lived in her home for nearly fifty years. It's full of a lifetime of memories, mementos, and personal items. Decades of memories mean it can be hard to leave.

The bones of the house are good; the property just needs some updating.

The decision now is whether she would rather sell her home "as-is" to a cash buyer *or* take the time in Salt Lake to get the home ready for a traditional sale.

Every situation has an emotional price tag, some more than others.

This is a big part of the price element. It compares the physical and mental stress of a traditional sale versus the convenience and clarity of a cash sale.

In this situation, the seller and her family need to consider:

- Postponing Mom's new life in Florida to clean out the house

- The financial cost of the daughter coming out to help with the house

- The physical and mental effort of vetting and hiring a contractor to update the house for the market, and managing the entire process

- The time it takes to put a home on the market

You can see there is a direct connection between selling at a lower monetary price with a lower emotional cost.

Every situation has an emotional price tag, some more than others.

A traditional sale may yield more money, but it also increases the time commitment and decreases the certainty of a sale.

FOUR EMOTIONAL COSTS TO CONSIDER

Certainty

Every situation is different, so the seller needs to decide what level of uncertainty they are prepared to accept. A traditional sale may yield more money, but it also increases the time commitment and decreases the certainty of a sale.

There is certainty in selling your home to a cash buyer, being able to communicate with them directly, and having a set closing date in the near future. Knowing a property is going to close on a specific date can provide the seller with a light at the end of a very dark tunnel.

Convenience

What is convenience worth for the family who lives in Florida and needs to sell Mom's house in Utah? Convenience for them is a lot more than just getting a fair cash offer for the property.

Convenience comes at a cost

Their convenience includes:

- Fewer travel costs across the country to prep for the sale

- Not having to sort and clean out the entire home

- Being able to move on with their lives without weeks or months of preparation

- Not having the added expenses of updates and repairs to a home they are leaving

- Knowing for sure they have a buyer and a closing date in hand

Convenience comes at a cost; the seller needs to know if it's worth it to them to skip the traditional sales route and the headaches that come with it.

Ease

It's difficult to put a price on the ease of a cash sale. With a cash sale, the seller is looking at a quick turnaround of days or weeks—not months.

The seller can show their potential cash buyer the property once. They are not faced with open houses, individual showings for multiple people, appraisals, inspections, repairs, renegotiations, and concessions.

A cash sale is designed to be short and sweet.

A cash sale is designed to be short and sweet.

Peace of Mind

There is a profound peace of mind that comes with being able to close one chapter of our lives and move on to the next.

Peace of mind comes from the certainty, ease, and convenience a cash sale gives to sellers. For our mother-daughter duo looking to start a new life in Florida, peace of mind in an already emotional process is priceless.

They will know Mom's house sold for a fair price. The daughter won't need to pause her own life to fly across the country to help Mom clean out and prepare to put the house on the market.

Instead, Mom can pack up what she wants, take that time to say goodbye to family and friends, and kick off her new life in the Sunshine State.

A cash buyer can provide clarity on the finances from the very beginning of the process. But only the seller knows the emotional price tag that certainty, convenience, ease, and peace of mind can provide. Every situation has a different value for these things, so it's really only something the seller can decide.

MORE THAN THE MONEY

Money is always going to be important in real estate, but it shouldn't always be the most important. Sellers should very much aim for a fair price for their property, but they also need to consider the emotional cost.

Often a seller puts too much weight on the money without considering the load of the emotions. Going back to Julia's story in Chapter 2, you can see so many elements of what we've talked about here. Her situation is one I'm trying to help others avoid.

She was so focused on the monetary price and the potential of getting $80,000 more that she ignored the emotional price that came along with it.

> **Only the seller knows the emotional price tag that certainty, convenience, ease, and peace of mind can provide.**

Julia and her husband faced an emotional cost with the buyers backing out just two days after having her father-in-law's funeral. They were dealing with the emotions of losing a loved one when the buyers came back to say they were going to give them $50,000 less than their original offer.

That uncertainty and stress is an emotional price. Having to restart the process of selling with a new buyer is an emotional price. The extra time it took for them to go through this process added an emotional price.

The purpose of this key is to understand the financial part of selling a home, but that the overall price for a seller has to consider the emotional costs as well. It's a balance.

RED FLAGS

- The red flags for this chapter are really more for you to consider. Before you decide to accept an offer-or really even to consider a cash sale-think about the emotional cost of the sale.

- Be honest with yourself about what's important to you.

- Make your best decision and move forward.

- Remember, selling your home is a big deal. Do your best to give it the time and consideration it needs so you can make the best choice for you.

THE BIG IDEA UNLOCKED

- If money is the most important thing for a seller, they are better off putting their house on the market and listing it traditionally with a real estate agent. If they are looking for convenience, certainty, ease, and peace of mind, then an as-is cash sale can provide that.

- While money is important, money isn't everything.

- You have to consider the emotional price of your sale. Know what these things are worth to you in your situation.

- For some people, it's worth a lot. For others, it's not worth as much. Take the time to consider what is best for you in your current situation and find the balance.

While money is
important, money isn't
everything.

PART TWO PUNCH LIST

Key Takeaways

- Earnest money needs to be non-refundable (at the very least after contingencies are removed).

- The higher the earnest money, the more serious the buyer.

- Know how much it costs to sell your home when it comes to title and escrow fees, real estate fees and commissions, taxes, and other costs.

- Know the amount of money you should be walking away with at the end of the sale.

- Use your Net Offer Equation to make an informed decision.

Offer Price - Debt = Net

- Money is important, but it isn't everything.

- There is an emotional cost to selling a home.

- Be sure to consider both the emotional cost and the financial cost when considering a cash offer.

PART TWO RED FLAGS

- If a buyer is hesitant to put down earnest money or wants to put down only a small amount, be cautious.

- If a buyer doesn't want earnest money to be nonrefundable, it could be a sign they aren't an experienced buyer.

- Keep an eye on fees and commissions.

- Not considering the emotional costs of selling a home could cost more financially and emotionally in the long run.

Want to learn more about what part money plays in a cash offer?

Scan the QR code and watch Paul's video.

1-800 BUY-HOUSES

SCAN ME

PART THREE

TIME

9

CONTINGENCY

"Has the Buyer Added Unnecessary Contingencies?"

"Paul stepped in when the first investor dropped out and with less then a week to close, kept the same closing date, and things went smoothly!"

—Carriene P.

In every friend group there seems to be that one person who always backs out of plans at the last minute. No matter how much preparation or advanced scheduling went into a meal or activity, they will always find a reason to not show.

You know the kind. Everyone plans to meet for dinner and a movie, but this person hits traffic or has to work late. Perhaps they even initiated the get-together and still manage to find a way to bail.

It can often lead to a waste of time and money for anyone left waiting. There is even a term for it called "mirage friend." They seem interested in engaging, but are they really?

These relationships are really frustrating. Mirage friends send the signal that your time is not important, other things take priority over you, and the whole thing feels disrespectful.

Ultimately, you have two choices—never make plans with them again, or accept the fact that they will continue to cancel.

No one wants a team member who never shows. They may seem enthusiastic about a project, but they never seem to follow through on the execution—again, wasting other people's time and money.

You certainly wouldn't go to an investor who was this way with your money, and you *definitely* don't want to get caught in a real estate contract with them.

These buyers manage their risk or lack of experience by providing themselves the opportunity to back out of the purchase contract at any time. They build in contingencies or clauses to the contract to give themselves the ability to walk away.

SPOTTING THE MIRAGE

The mirage buyer seems great at first. They are enthusiastic about your property and all the potential. They make big promises and offer to purchase the property for the exact amount or close to your asking price. They are sure they can close quickly without any hiccups.

> **You can always tell if a cash buyer is legitimate by what they put in the contract.**

These buyers talk big but usually fail to deliver.

These buyers manage their risk or lack of experience by providing themselves the opportunity to back out of the purchase contract at any time. They build in contingencies or clauses to the contract to give themselves the ability to walk away in the event that they aren't able to find a buyer (wholesaler) or don't like what they see in a future home inspection.

So how is a seller supposed to recognize the difference between a mirage buyer and the real deal? Well, the proof is in the pudding—or in this case, the contract.

You can always tell if a cash buyer is legitimate *by what they put in the contract.*

Sellers who understand contingencies put themselves in the best possible position to accept the right cash offer. If left unchecked, contingencies can put the seller in a bind.

I recently spoke with a homeowner who was in the final stages of a divorce. It was time for him to start a new chapter in his life, which included selling his home of over ten years.

As any good homeowner would, he reached out to several cash buyers. To this seller's credit, he was more thorough than many homeowners, and he carefully read the purchase agreement. The purchase price of the offers he had received seemed fair, but something didn't feel right.

The further he read, the more uncomfortable he became because of the contingencies he noticed in the purchase contract. The most glaring contingency was a **twenty-one-day home inspection** period with the **close of escrow** to happen on or before twenty-one days.

So what does that mean exactly? That means the buyer could potentially walk away from the purchase of the home up until the day the property was supposed to close *at no risk to the buyer*. It was a lopsided contract. The buyer could simply call him up on the morning of the closing and say they aren't going to purchase the property.

Thankfully this seller understood the importance of contingencies and avoided putting himself at a severe disadvantage.

UNDERSTANDING CONTINGENCIES

A *contingency* is defined as "a provision or unforeseen event or circumstance." In typical real estate transactions, contingencies provide protection and flexibility by allowing both the buyer and seller to avoid risks.

When it comes to a cash offer from a cash homebuyer, though, things change.

In this situation, contingencies are great for buyers—these loopholes give them all the power. For sellers, however, they introduce uncertainty and potential delays. Buyers use contingencies to their advantage, strategically applying them for any "unforeseen circumstance" to back out of an agreement.

The most common contingencies are:

- Home Inspections (most common)
- Appraisals (we will discuss this later)
- Financing
- Sale of Current Home
- HOA

THE CONTRACT

When it comes to the actual purchase agreement, each state has a different real estate purchase contract with different elements of contingencies. While these contingencies may vary, they are all very similar regardless of location.

The most common contingency when considering a cash offer is the home inspection. For this reason, our focus will remain on the inspection contingency and understanding the ins and outs of it. This clause allows the buyer to have a home inspected within a set time period. Should the buyer not like the results, they can back out of the contract. Here's an example of how that might look:

> **Inspection Period***: Buyer's obligations to close this transaction are subject to the satisfaction of a buyer's investigation inspection of the property. Buyer shall have fourteen days from the date of this agreement during which time buyer will have the* **absolute right to cancel this agreement for any reason whatsoever** *at buyer's sole and absolute discretion.*

To cut through all of the real estate jargon, this says that the buyer has the right for two weeks to get a home inspection and perform due diligence on the property. For the buyer, that's two weeks to decide if they want to purchase the property or wholesale the property, and if either of those options don't work out, the buyer has the right to simply cancel the contract.

For you, the seller, those fourteen days leave you in limbo, and oftentimes you don't even know it.

THE CONTINGENCY PERIOD

Buyers will often try to give themselves as much time as possible in this due diligence period. As the seller, this time period is crucial. The fewer number of days allowed in this contingency, the less likely the buyer is to back out. It also keeps the entire process moving forward.

A legitimate cash buyer can waive contingencies in *forty-eight hours or less.*

> The fewer number of days allowed in this contingency, the less likely the buyer is to back out.

LESSONS LEARNED THE HARD WAY

Julia learned this the hard way when she accepted an incredibly high cash offer *laden with contingencies*. She later told us that our offer wasn't the second or even third highest.

"We had a few higher offers, but the lack of all contingencies has to be considered more than I did originally," Julia said. During the contingency period, her original agreement was renegotiated down and was no longer the prize amount it originally seemed.

In the end, the offer fell through and left her and her husband back at square one. The lesson is clear: Don't give buyers any more time than necessary to remove contingencies.

RED FLAGS

- When contingencies are removed within two days, it puts the seller in the best position to maintain the original offer price and closing date.

- This quick turnaround has the added benefit of cutting out any renegotiations.

- If used correctly contingencies can provide the seller a significant amount of certainty.

- If the buyer needs more than forty-eight hours to remove ALL contingencies it's a big red flag.

THE BIG IDEA UNLOCKED

- If you're a buyer, you want as many contingencies as possible.

- If you're a seller, you want as few contingencies as possible.

- In an effort to be fair to both parties in a cash offer situation, I've found a good balance in having a forty-eight-hour time frame.

- Experienced cash buyers should be able to remove all contingencies within forty-eight hours of signing the purchase agreement. This gives the buyer time to evaluate any major concerns on their end, while still providing the seller with the peace of mind that their home is under contract and the sale is definite.

- As the seller, you want to limit the number of loopholes and cap the contingency time frame to forty-eight hours. It will increase your confidence in the buyer and certainty that the offer will close in the time you want.

When contingencies are removed within two days, it puts the seller in the best position to maintain the original offer price and closing date.

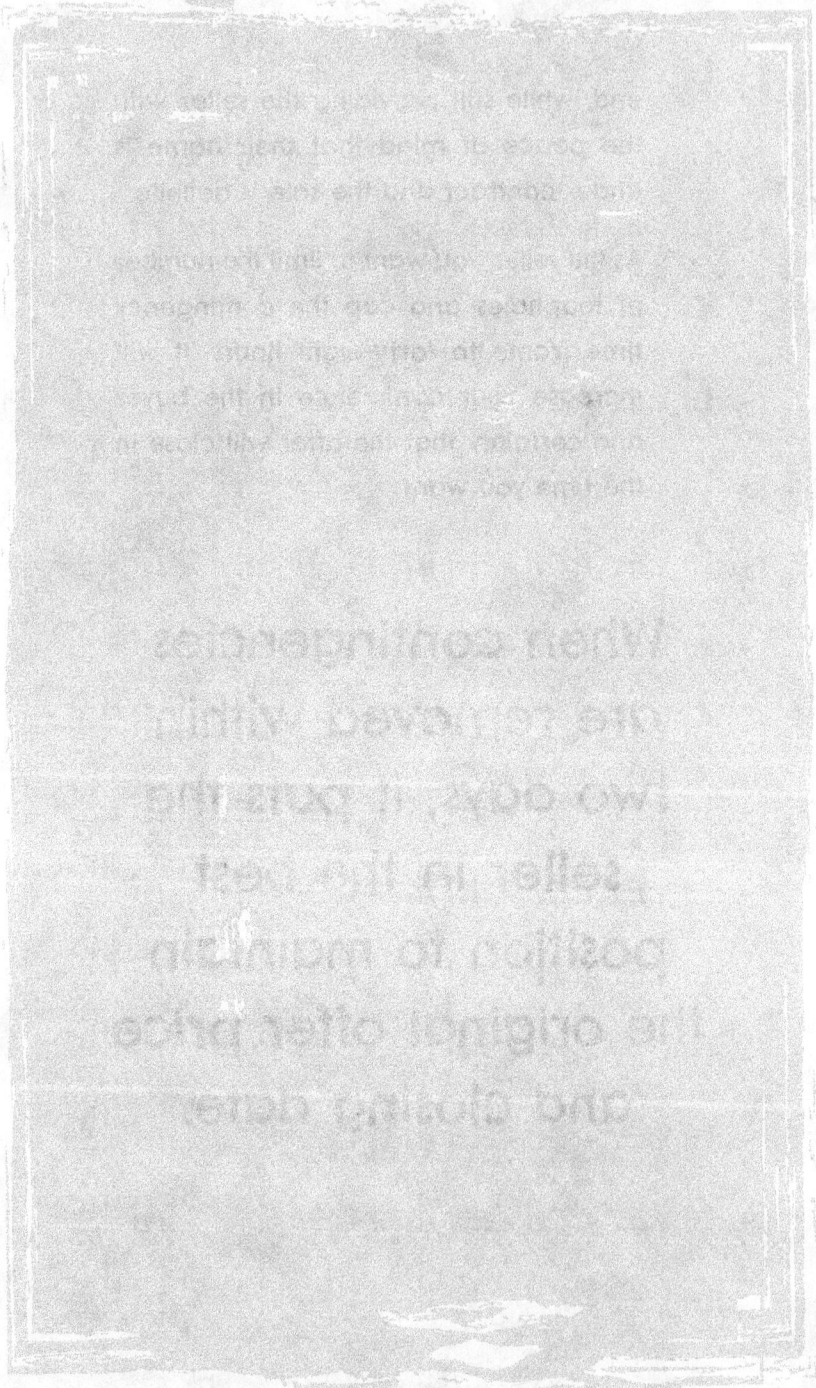

10
APPRAISAL

"Is the Buyer Willing to Skip an Appraisal to Move Quickly?"

"Selling my house to Paul Baird was the least stressful and fastest process I have ever dealt with when selling a home... It was so nice to be able to talk to him on Monday and already have the sale completed with funds only four days later on a Friday!"

—Derek L.

Have you ever had someone try to sell you something you don't need? Maybe they are pressuring you to add all the bells and whistles to your new car. Perhaps they are trying to convince you that one waffle maker just isn't enough. They may even be trying to sell you another dozen boxes of Girl Scout cookies.

We've all seen the advertisements and heard the jokes about the pressure the time-share industry puts on potential customers. Even sitcoms use it as a situational trope. More than one show has seen a well-meaning dad sign the family up for a free, all-expenses-paid vacation, only to spend most of the time avoiding the sales pitch.

The truth is that an appraisal is not needed when working with an experienced cash buyer.

Regardless of the product someone is pushing, it can get a little tough to stand firm and say, "No!" You don't want to be the bad guy. You're not looking to insult anybody; you just want to make the purchase and be done.

Saying no can be uncomfortable, especially in situations where you're not completely confident in the details.

Sellers may be put in a situation where buyers try to convince them to agree to things they don't really need. And saying no is exactly what they need to do.

Some cash buyers will try to do an **appraisal** on the property.

They may insist that this is a normal part of real estate, and while it is normal in a traditional real estate transaction, in an all-cash offer from an experienced homebuyer, it is completely unnecessary. These buyers are banking on the fact that the seller won't know that.

The truth is that *an appraisal is not needed when working with an experienced cash buyer.*

ASSESSING THE SITUATION

Simply put, an **appraisal** is done in order to determine the value of the property.

In a traditional real estate transaction, the buyer goes to a bank or mortgage broker to get a loan. They apply for a mortgage in order to borrow money to purchase a property.

The lender wants to limit risk. To do that, they need to know the actual value of the property being purchased. They don't want to lend $200,000 on a property that's worth $100,000. Based on the appraised value of the property, the lender then decides how much to loan the buyer. Traditional mortgage lenders will lend 80-90% of a property's **appraised value.**

Real estate appraisals are performed by licensed third parties not connected with the lender. These third-party appraisers' job is to determine the value of the property and report back to the lender.

The appraiser will visit the property to determine the property's square footage, bedrooms and bathrooms, and overall condition, along with other factors such as the area and current market conditions. They will then determine the value of the property.

If an appraisal is done and does not come back at the value the buyer was expecting, the buyer can use this to their advantage.

An appraisal can become a tool for the buyer to renegotiate the agreed-upon price. Since the buyer won't be able to borrow the amount of money needed to meet the original purchase amount, they may not have enough money to make up the difference between the agreed purchase price and the required down payment.

Anything a seller can do to eliminate the risk of roadblocks increases the likelihood of the transaction closing smoothly and improves the seller's position of getting the original agreed-upon price.

While these appraisals are important and necessary to traditional real estate transactions, they are completely unnecessary when working with an experienced cash buyer.

If your goal is to work with a seasoned cash buyer, avoid buyers who claim to need appraisals or financing contingencies.

Experienced cash buyers will have the cash in hand or access to cash without having to do an appraisal on the property.

Experienced cash buyers will have the cash in hand or access to cash without having to do an appraisal on the property. There are very few reasons a lender would need to be involved and an appraisal done. Should a buyer insist on getting an appraisal, be sure to understand why, or walk away.

HARD MONEY

A common financing technique used by some cash buyers is called hard money. Hard money loans are short-term loans given at a higher interest rate to a cash buyer based strictly on the value of the property. Because these loans tend to be riskier, a lender can charge a borrower more interest with the expectation that the borrower has the ability to add value to the property and sell it for a profit.

Anytime an appraisal is requested on a property, it provides more uncertainty for the seller.

A lot of cash buyers use hard money loans to purchase properties since there is a quick turnaround. However, hard money lenders are still in the business of making money and reducing risk. They want to know they are making good loans, so they can also require an appraisal.

Anytime an appraisal is requested on a property, it provides more uncertainty for the seller—potentially resulting in the buyer having to reduce the purchase price and extend the closing date. To gauge the value of a property, appraisers consider not just the condition of the property but the overall conditions of the real estate market, which could affect the value of the property. This can create a number of scenarios that cost the seller time and money.

Part of the property's evaluation includes the consideration of comparable homes in the area. Unfortunately, this can mean that much of your home's value is outside of your control. While appraisers do their best to determine the correct value based on the market, there can sometimes be a difference of opinion on what someone is willing to pay and what the appraisers think it is worth.

Sellers should strive for a cash offer that doesn't include loan and appraisal contingencies.

This means buyers can use appraisals to renegotiate their original offer or just walk away from the offer altogether.

Sellers should strive for a cash offer that doesn't include loan and appraisal contingencies. This will assure the seller that their buyer has the cash on hand and is not at risk of the transaction not going through based on a third party's estimation.

RED FLAGS

- Appraisals are an important part of the majority of real estate transactions, but not when it comes to cash offers.

- Be hesitant to allow an appraisal contingency in the purchase agreement.

- Many investors use hard money to purchase properties. Understand that depending on the hard money lenders opinion on value it could affect your bottom line.

- Appraisals take time. Bank and lender approvals take time. As the seller, you want to have the peace of mind and certainty that the house is going to close when the buyer says. Remember, the contingency element. If there's an appraisal contingency, someone else has to sign off on the sale, which creates a hurdle for the seller.

- Under very few circumstances should a cash buyer be allowed to do an appraisal on the property,

11

CLOSING

"Can the Buyer Make the Closing Happen in the Next Seven Days?"

"Paul promptly came out the same afternoon...and he came prepared with the information he needed to make a decision... The next day the title company emailed a payoff form for me, and once I returned it, an hour later, set up a closing date for the next business day."

— Mike M.

The space between when you've made a decision and when the effects take place can sometimes be the slowest time in the world.

Think about when you've booked a vacation...and then have to wait six months to take it. Or you've decided to change jobs...but have to give your notice and wait two weeks to leave. Or you decide to get married...but the wedding is next year.

Tom Petty sang that *the waiting is the hardest part*—and he was not wrong.

In real estate, the payoff and grand finale are at the closing table. This is when you complete the transaction of selling your house. The buyer gets the keys, and you get your money. When you've been through the wringer with tenants or had to deal with cross-country travel to handle a home that needs to be sold, the **close of escrow** can't come soon enough.

That's why the buyer's ability to close in seven days is so important.

The big draw of an all-cash offer is the promise of swift action

SHORT AND SWEET

The big draw of an all-cash offer is *the promise of swift action* in a process that can sometimes take up to two or three months. With this in mind, an experienced cash buyer should have no problem closing a real estate transaction in seven to ten days.

While a seven-day timeline isn't a hard and fast rule—the closing period is something that is 100% dependent on the seller's wishes—most people we talk to are looking to close sooner rather than later.

I tell homeowners that we can close on a property as soon as the title work is done, which, if necessary, can be done in three or four days, but we've also closed houses in weeks or months. It is up to the *seller* in these situations to advocate for how quickly the sale will go, depending on their needs.

Whether or not the seller chooses to close in seven to ten days, the buyer should have *the ability to do so*.

Why? Because, if the buyer can close in seven days, that means:

1. They're likely removing all contingencies within forty-eight hours.

2. There's no time for an appraisal.

3. They've got the money.

The buyer's ability to close this soon offers the seller confidence that the cash offer will most likely go through.

RED FLAGS

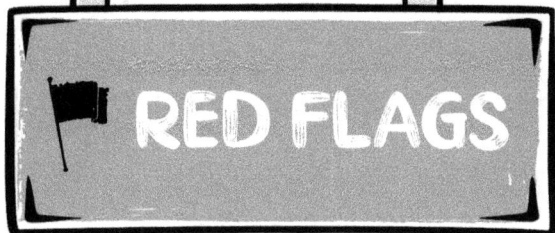

If a buyer insists that five to seven days is too fast for a closing, consider the next buyer.

Not being able to meet this tight deadline means the buyer is missing one of the key criteria. It could be a sign that they:

- Don't have the cash and are borrowing, meaning they need time for appraisals and loan approvals.

- Are intending to assign the contract to someone else.

- Are hoping to renegotiate the price down from the original offer.

None of these reasons are good for the certainty and peace of mind of the seller.

- To be fair, seven days is a pretty fast turnaround. Most people want to close in two to three weeks, but this is all about the buyer's ability to close quickly. It is evidence that they have been honest and authentic cash buyers.

- Make sure your buyer is legitimate and can meet the closing time frame that works best for you by asking for proof of funds. This is not difficult for an experienced cash buyer to do. They should have relationships with the title and escrow company to get the paperwork in order in case you are looking for a quick turnaround.

- The buyer's ability to close in such a short amount of time provides confidence to the seller that they can focus on starting the next chapter of their lives.

PART THREE PUNCH LIST

Key Takeaways

- Contingencies benefit the buyer far more than the seller.

- Limit the number of contingencies, and never allow more than forty-eight hours.

- An appraisal contingency should be considered as a major red flag.

- Appraisals can be a waste of time and open the door to renegotiations.

- Aim for a quick closing.

- The buyer should have the ability to close in five to seven days.

- Closing timeline should be dependent on the seller's needs, not the buyer's.

- Ask for proof of funds.

PART THREE RED FLAGS

- Watch out for buyers needing more than a forty-eight-hour contingency period.

- Try to avoid buyers who claim to need appraisals or financing contingencies.

- Skip the buyer who insists that a five-to seven-day closing is too fast.

Want to learn more about time in a cash offer?

Scan the QR code with your phone camera and watch Paul's video.

1-800 BUY-HOUSES

SCAN ME

12

A WORD ABOUT FORECLOSURES

The word foreclosure sounds intimidating. It can obviously be more intimidating when you are in the process of one. The uncertainty someone feels when going through the foreclosure process can be both financially and emotionally exhausting. I have spoken with countless homeowners who are understandably confused, uneducated, and scared about what to do next. It's not a fun situation, and I sympathize with anyone who has had to experience it.

Lenders are in the business of lending money, not owning real estate.

WHAT IS A FORECLOSURE?

Foreclosure is a legal process in which a lender or bank attempts to recover the balance of a loan from a borrower who has stopped making payments. In other words, if a homeowner stops paying what they agreed to pay when they purchased the home, the lender has a right to foreclose and recover any money owed.

Lenders are in the business of lending money, not owning real estate. But in order to recover any money owed, lenders must go through the foreclosure process. The final step of that process is a public auction, where the bank is either going to sell the property to a third party (anyone willing to pay what the bank is asking), or the bank is going to repossess the property and sell it on the open market. Either way, the bank is going to try and recover as much money as possible up to the amount it loaned.

WHAT IS THAT PROCESS?

In a perfect world, lenders and banks don't want to own real estate; they want to loan money and collect interest. But when the borrower doesn't make payments as promised, there are certain steps a lender needs to follow in order to collect what is owed to them.

So how long does that process take?

While the foreclosure process varies slightly from state to state, all of them require public notices as well as notification to all parties that the property is in foreclosure and could be going up for auction.

Typically after three to six months of missed payments, the lender will file a notice called a notice of default (NOD) with the county recorder. This notice officially states that the borrower has defaulted on the mortgage, and the property will soon be scheduled for auction. If the borrower isn't proactive between the time the notice of default is filed and the sale date, the lender will either sell the property or take possession of the property.

The U.S. Department of Housing and Urban Development—known popularly as HUD—says this on its website: It's important to note that even though foreclosure doesn't start for months, lender fees and penalties start when payments are only ten to fifteen days late.[1]

---

[1]   https://www.hud.gov/topics/avoiding_foreclosure/foreclosureprocess

The most important thing a borrower can do is be proactive about the situation.

In short, a lender can foreclose on a property in as little as six months, but it could also take as long as two years. The most important thing a borrower can do is be proactive about the situation. I have seen countless homeowners procrastinate in taking action, and that results in losing their homes. The saddest situations are when something could have been done but wasn't.

So what are the options if you find yourself in foreclosure?

THREE OPTIONS

Option 1

Pay the bank what's owed. If you've missed five payments, pay the five payments with the interest and penalties. This makes the loan current and as if nothing ever happened. It sounds really simple to just pay what you owe, but obviously is easier said than done.

If you do not have the money, selling the property might be the best option. Depending on the circumstances, selling the property before the auction date could pay off the lender, stop the foreclosure, and put money in your pocket. This is sometimes hard for homeowners to understand

and can be a very emotional situation. While this option is often met with some hesitancy, it is sometimes the best thing to do. Sell the home, get the money you can, and move on with life.

The most common mistake people make is they spend too much time trying to find ways to save a house they can't afford when they should be spending their time trying to sell the house to maximize the equity.

Option 2

Do a loan modification. A loan modification is basically telling the bank you can no longer afford the payments and need to renegotiate the loan. These were much more common five or six years ago, but are still an option today. Again, the bank doesn't want your house. They don't want to own real estate. They just want to receive the money they were promised. Let them know you want to stay in your house and would like to work something out while you're experiencing this financial hardship. They may be willing to do a loan modification.

The roadblock here is that some homeowners won't qualify for a loan modification. It could be because they don't have employment, too much personal debt, or various other reasons.

But if you do qualify, it can be a really good option.

Take the following example: Let's say you lost your job for five to six months and were unable to make any mortgage payments during that time. Then you found a new job that allows you to make those payments today. This is a situation that would make sense for both the borrower and lender to work something out. Talk with the lender and see what options are available. Many homeowners don't realize that doing a modification to their loan is even possible. It is, and it should be pursued.

Option 3

It's a complicated one—filing for bankruptcy. This is a choice that homeowners often choose because it can give them more time in the property (short term) but it doesn't really solve the problem. It kicks the can (problem) down the road. Bankruptcy is taking your debt and trying to reorganize it in a way that you can afford. When you file for bankruptcy, it pauses the foreclosure. The foreclosure process will stop until a judge looks at your situation, specifically your debts, and either says, "Yes" or "No" to moving forward with the bankruptcy.

> **Filing for bankruptcy can give homeowners more time in the property (short term) but it doesn't really solve the problem.**

In my experience, a lot of people in foreclosure treat filing for bankruptcy like a band-aid. It rarely fixes the problem. It slows the bleeding, but it doesn't heal the wound. Countless times I have seen a borrower file for bankruptcy in a foreclosure situation, postponing the foreclosure for several months, only to see the foreclosure happening again in six to eight months.

I'm not saying that it's a bad option for some people. But, it is a bad option for people who are just looking to postpone the sale and not solve the real problem.

So, if you're facing foreclosure or it's a near possibility, it's important to understand and evaluate your current financial situation. Can you actually afford the house?

- If you feel like you went through a time period that was a little bit difficult financially, but you can make your payments now, maybe the loan modification is what is best for you.

- If you have a bunch of other debt and feel like you could handle it if you were able to rearrange it, get an attorney's advice and see what they have to say.

- Then finally, if you can't afford a house but you have equity in it, you may be able to maximize your equity by selling it. A sale will likely allow you to pay off your mortgage without ruining your credit and even walk away with something to get you started on the next chapter in your life.

Every situation is different, but these general guidelines can help you make a more informed decision about what is right for you and your family.

13
CONCLUSION

Regardless of the circumstances that bring you to sell your home for cash—whether you've inherited property, are retiring as a landlord, are moving, or are trying to get out from under a mountain of debt—accepting a quick, all-cash offer can free you up to move on to the next chapter of your life.

While the process of selling a home can be overwhelming, using the tools you've learned here can reduce the stress of working with the wrong cash buyer and help you gauge an offer that is right for you. It has been my goal in this book to provide transparency to the homeowner who is considering a cash offer.

Using the tools
you've learned
here can reduce
the stress of
working with
the wrong cash
buyer and help
you gauge an
offer that is
right for you.

The principles discussed in this book are ones I have personally used for over fifteen years as a cash buyer.

Keeping the best interest of the homeowner in mind, I am certain I have missed out on opportunities because I have stayed true to these principles. That's okay. I'd rather live with integrity and help people make the best decision.

Homeowners deserve the truth, and that's been the purpose of this book.

I have purposely tried to expose the smoke and mirrors that are often prevalent among cash buyers. Homeowners deserve the truth, and that's been the purpose of this book.

As you have read through each part, it is my hope that it has provided understanding and clarity that

- A cash offer is not right for everyone.

- Vetting the experience of the buyer will reveal their real intent with the property.

- Price is more than just how much money you walk away with—you have to consider the emotional cost.

- Timeframes within the purchase agreement need to benefit the seller more than the buyer.

When a homeowner understands these four principles, I am confident they will be able to make an informed decision. I hope you will use this book as a guide and resource throughout your decision-making process. From my perspective, the greatest compliment I can receive from a homeowner is, "Paul, thank you for your honesty."

Please feel free to visit 1800BuyHouses.com for more free resources and content. Also please don't hesitate to contact me directly at paulbaird@1800BuyHouses.com.

The Perfect Cash Offer™

CONTINGENCY
All contingencies removed within 48 hours of signed purchase agreement.

APPRAISAL
No appraisal contingency.

CLOSING
Buyer has the ABILITY to close in 7 days or less.

EARNEST MONEY
Non-refundable earnest money at the time of acceptance or at least after all contingencies are removed within 48 hours of acceptance.

NET OFFER
NET PROCEEDS (NET=NO EXTRA THINGS.)

PRICE
Consider both purchase price ($$$) and the emotional price of the sale.

AUTHORITY
Work directly with the ultimate decision maker (eliminate the middlemen).

REFERENCE
Research the buyer by talking with previous clients and affiliated title and escrow companies, and evaluating their online presence.

EXPERIENCE
Work with an experienced cash buyer.

1-800 BUY-HOUSES®

BUYER

AUTHORITY–Work only with the person that has the ultimate authority and ability to purchase your property. (eliminate middlemen)

EXPERIENCE–Verify that the prospective buyer has previous experience buying houses for cash.

REFERENCE–Do research on the buyer by talking with previous clients, evaluating their online presence and talking with the title and escrow company they work with.

MONEY

EARNEST MONEY–Require non-refundable earnest money at the time of acceptance or at least after all contingencies are removed within 48 hours of acceptance.

NET OFFER–Know the exact amount you will be walking away with at closing. NET. NO EXTRA THINGS.

PRICE–Consider both purchase price ($$$) and the emotional price of the sale. Find the balance between the two for your specific situation.

TIME

CONTINGENCY–Remove all contingencies within 48 hours.

APPRAISAL–Do not allow an appraisal contingency.

CLOSING–Make sure the buyer has the ABILITY to close in 7 days or less.

LEGAL DISCLOSURE: The information presented herein represents the view of the author as of the date of publication. This book is presented for informational purposes only. While every attempt has been made to verify the information in this book, the author assumes no responsibility for errors, inaccuracies, or omissions.

This publication comes with the understanding that the author is not engaged in rendering legal, accounting, financial, or other professional service. If legal advice or other expert assistance is required, the services of a competent professional person should be sought.

GLOSSARY

Appraisal—A third party's estimate of the value of a property

Asking Price—The amount of money a homeowner is asking for a property

Assignable Contracts—A purchase agreement that gives the buyer the right to assign or transfer his interest to another party

Assignment Fee—The difference between what the seller was promised and what the actual buyer is paying

Cash Buyer—Someone who uses their own money to cover the full purchase price of a property

Closing—The day the seller and buyer transfer title to the property and money changes hands

Contingencies—A way out of the contract for the buyer

Earnest Money—A good-faith deposit from the buyer that shows they intend to purchase the property

Emotional Price—The amount of mental and emotional stress a seller can feel surrounding the sale of a property

Escrow Company—A third party who holds and handles the money in a real estate transaction.

Financing—Providing funds for the purchase of real estate, typically provided by a lender or bank

Hard Money—Private, short-term loans buyers will use to "flip" a property, typically comes with a higher interest rate

Home Inspections Contingency—Gives the buyer the right to have the home inspected in a specific time period

Judgments—A line that gives a creditor the right to be paid a certain amount of money from the proceeds of the sale of a property

MLS (Multi-Listing Service)—A resource (online) to help listing agents and brokers find other cooperative agents and brokers who are working with buyers to sell their clients properties or homes, created by the National Association of REALTORS®

Net Offer—Amount of money the buyer offers for the property without fees and commissions

Net Proceeds—Amount of money the seller is left with at the end of the sale

Real Estate Agent—A person who represents homebuyers and sellers during sales. They are licensed, work off commission, and are guided by federal and state rules and regulations. They are required to disclose that they are working with a party to broker a real estate transaction.

Real Estate Attorney—An attorney who is present at the closing of a real estate transaction. Some states require the physical presence of an attorney at closing.

Title Company—Third party who does research on the title of the property and who issues title insurance

Wholesaler—Person or company who acts as a middleman in the sale of a home

www.ingramcontent.com/pod-product-compliance
Lightning Source LLC
Chambersburg PA
CBHW071233210326
41597CB00016B/2031